Creative Writing Wps for Children

Denise Howie

Warning - Disclaimer

The purpose of this book is to provide guidelines to help teach creative writing and/or to be able to write more creatively. The author shall have neither liability nor responsibility to any person or entity with respect to any loss or damage caused, or alleged to have been caused, directly or indirectly, by the information contained in this book.

For
Jack, Ric & Mary

Table of Contents

PART THREE

Wise Words: Insightful writing quotes

Foreword by Maureen Almond

In her introduction Denise Howie explains how she has tutored potential writers between the ages of 5 and 84. Denise was my first ever writing tutor and although I was not 84, I was of mature years I owe my life as a published poet largely to Denise who encouraged my first very tentative steps into creative writing.

When I first joined Denise's class I had not done any creative writing at all and I initially went to her classes with a view to learning how to develop magazine articles. When she decided to introduce poetry into her workshops I was terrified and took her aside telling her that I knew nothing at all about the subject and felt very afraid of it; I was ready to drop out of the class. But Denise has a very gentle, encouraging way with students, she persuaded me to continue with the group and to embrace the poetry reading and writing exercises that she would give. It was one of the very best things I have ever done.

Long after Denise moved from England I continued with my writing, continued attending classes and eventually took an MA in writing poetry at the University of Newcastle. I have recently submitted a PhD thesis on the subject of usefulness in poetry with particular reference to the Roman Poet, Horace. I have six collections of poetry published and my work is on the recommended reading list for classics students at Oxford University who are studying reception of the classics.

But this is not about me, this is about Denise Howie – without her wide knowledge and gentle friendly help and support in those early days I would have achieved none of these things. I would say to anyone who is interested in developing their creative writing skills that they could do no better than follow the lead and advice provided by Denise.

Happy writing to all!
Maureen Almond

Maureen Almond is a respected poet who brings together Latin poets and the characters and culture of her northern upbringing. (N.E. England.) Her work is included in the Primary Texts Reading List for the Oxford University Course, *The Reception of Classical Literature in Twentieth-Century Poetry in English* and has been cited in *The Cambridge Companion to Horace* (2007).

About the Author

Denise Howie currently resides in British Columbia, Canada. She has over twenty years of experience in running creative writing workshops for children and adults and has won a number of awards for her poetry and fiction, including winner of the Australia / New Zealand section of the Commonwealth Short Story Contest. Her short film 'The Girl in the Lay-by' was nominated for a BAFTA and won best short film in the Las Palmas Film Festival.

Denise has had success as a playwright and her short stories have been broadcast on BBC Radio. She has been published in magazines and newspapers in Britain, New Zealand and Canada.

Denise also uses her writing skills to raise funds and awareness for The One Person Project, a grass roots organization that is in the process of helping a community in East-Africa to become self-sustaining.

Acknowledgements

I wish to thank Sheena Fowlie for proof reading the *Creative Writing Workshops for Children* series.

I was extremely fortunate to spend the 1990's in the vibrant and creative arena of the Tees Valley in the North of England. I wish to acknowledge the many writers and writing activists of that time, especially writer and poet Andy Croft. I was privileged to be able to attend festivals, courses and workshops organized by a number of community arts projects, the Cleveland County Arts Council and New Writing North.

My rich writing education continued when I moved to Auckland and became a member of the New Zealand Writers Guild Foundation. I wish to acknowledge writer, director Christine Parker for mentoring me, Barrie Partridge and the screenwriting gang and the Auckland Arts Council and the Writers Guild.

I also wish to acknowledge and thank the children and youth who have taken part in the Writing for Fun workshops. So much enthusiasm! So many unique voices! It is a privilege to witness the alchemy of ideas and words and to be introduced to new characters and a freshly minted universe.

INTRODUCTION

Ask a child to share the daily adventures his favourite toys and you are likely to hear about fairy princesses, voyages to the moon, heroic battles and other exploits that put Buzz and Woody to shame.

A few years later the child will have great stories in his head but if asked to write them down the inventive words and scenarios often become diluted or fizzle out altogether, and so it continues through school, college and life. In fact studies show that our measurable creativity drops dramatically from age 3 to adulthood.

The aim of this book is to share the knowledge I have gained in twenty years of running *Writing for Fun* workshops for children and adults in which, both the students who love to write and those who hate it find their creative voice – and have fun in the process!

Many students fail to engage with the writing process because of the mechanical aspects of writing. These workshops focus on creativity, delaying the editing process until the piece is finished. I have found that when students have worked hard on building and restructuring a story or a poem they are more than willing to go through it one more time to add the final polish to make it ready for 'publication'.

As a reader and a writer I understand the power of words. As a writing tutor I have seen students from age 5 to 84 discover the power of their own words; it can be a transformative experience, especially for those who struggle to read and write or have lived a life believing that they have nothing worthwhile to say.

How to use this book

The book is about providing a safe and inspiring environment for students to express themselves through enhanced creative writing.

There are nine Level 1 *Writing For Fun* workshops and detailed lesson plans so that you can easily equip your students with the tools used by the world's leading writers and confidently provide exercises to hone their skills.

The workshops are designed to be used in order at your own pace. A 90 minute workshop would be ideal with a five to ten minute break in the middle, but the exercises work well in a 1 hour block with 40 minutes for the exercises and 20 minutes for class discussion, illustrations and opportunities for students to read out their work. The workshops can be easily split if your lessons are shorter, and there are additional exercises at the end of the book if you need to add an extra lesson or extend a workshop.

Part One discusses the building blocks of great writing.

Part Two contains lesson plans and student worksheets for the workshops, including an overview and list of objectives for each workshop if you require them. I have also included inspirational writing quotes.

Part Three contains extra writing exercises and examples, and covers editing for spelling, punctuation and grammar; advice on how to help young children and those who have challenges with writing, and a list of well-known people who have overcome reading and writing difficulties.

I use the same workshops for children and adults; the principles are the same whatever the participant's age.

How to get the best from your students

- Participate in the exercises yourself. Share the pride of creation.

- Make sure you carry out the 'banish the editor' instruction before every session.

- Make time for students to share ideas before writing and to read excerpts of their work at the end of the session – this can be done in groups in a large class. In the first session or two some students might be shy about sharing but I have found that by the end of the course even the most reticent are urging me to pick them first to read their work out loud! (Some students may prefer you to read their piece out for them, which is great – they are still sharing!)

- If a student is stuck help them out by asking questions – How is the character feeling? What does she hear? Etc.

- Children are always keen to illustrate their stories so allow a little time in the session and encourage the students to complete the picture at home.

- If available, you can use computers to complete the story after the brainstorming and exercises.

- Don't worry if a child is always writing about the same subject matter; it's an advantage to be emotionally engaged and create from a place of strong interest.

- Do not be alarmed if children include elements of death and violence in their work, it is perfectly natural, try to redirect rather than forbid content that you are not comfortable with, ask the student to explore a more creative and powerful alternative.

- Print off each student's finished collection. The pride of publication is a great incentive! In writing groups publish an anthology of everyone's best work.

- Have students sit under a table to write…

- Run the workshop outside…

- Enjoy watching students blossom as they discover new talents and strengthen old skills.

- Have fun!

The Building Blocks of Great Writing

By using the following concepts to teach creative writing you will absorb the skills of an award winning writer with over twenty-years of creative writing tutoring experience.

Teaching creative writing is less about spelling and grammar and more about giving students a voice. Allow students to explore creatively with words and language and they will be jumping out of their seats to share their work with the class!

All the words I use in my stories can be found in the dictionary -
it's just a matter of arranging them into the right sentences.
Somerset Maugham

Banish the Editor!

In the 1960s educator George Land was asked by NASA to develop a way to assess the creativity of its scientists and engineers. Land went on to use the same assessment tool to test the imaginative capabilities of children ages 3-5. He found that 98% of the children scored as 'creative geniuses', compared to just 2% of adults.

He tested the same 1,600 children again at five year intervals and found a massive drop in creativity, down to only 30% scoring highly at age 8-10, and just 12% at age13-15, and 2% at age 25.

Land observed that we start out creative and *learn* to be uncreative! (George Land and Beth Jarman – Breaking Point and Beyond.)

In the same way that Betty Edwards, *Drawing on the Right Side of the Brain*, urges us to ignore the logical, left side of our brain, I tell my students to ignore the Editor in their head, in fact I make them banish him or her for the duration of the class. Some children send their Editor off for a coffee at a local café (interestingly children usually perceive their inner editor to be older than they themselves are) whilst others might shred theirs through the building's ventilation system and send them on their way. (More on violence in children's writing in Level Two!)

You will be familiar with your own Editor, the voice that says, *You can't write that, it's stupid.* Or *That doesn't look right, that's not how you spell that word, how on earth do you spell it?* The very same Editor that is in cahoots with a host of nasty inner critics who can prevent you moving forward if you listen to them.

Introduce The Orator & The Sculptor!

Writing Free

During the following exercises and in the creative time afterwards, encourage students to just write, not to worry about spelling, not to stop and wonder if it makes sense. Not to care what other people might think. It is this hesitance that stunts our creativity.

The process will be counterintuitive for the students and for you – especially if you teach in a school setting. The child will ask how to spell a word and you will want to respond, after all that's what parents, teachers and workshop facilitators do – help the student to find the 'correct' way! Remind students to banish their Editor, allow them to discuss creative ways in which to get the interloper out of the building – it's all fuel to the storywriter's fire - but do of course help the child out if the spelling situation is causing stress.

Speak and Leap

For the first five or ten minutes of a writing session allow and encourage the students to talk, to get excited about their ideas and 'spark' off each other. It will get loud and it will get silly – good. Hopefully your own Editor will be paddling on a warm beach or cozied up reading a good book somewhere and you will appreciate the drama and humour being traded around the fire… I mean table. You will have your own guidelines for what is acceptable but try to redirect rather than cut off storylines. In the same way that the spoken word preceded the written, the opportunity to describe ideas out loud can help catapult the student into the story on the page.

Inevitably one child will borrow another's idea but this is a good opportunity to point out that even if a room full of writers all start off with the same story title or theme, they will each come up with a unique story. (There is no collective noun for writers – that would be a fun activity! A blurb of writers…a paraphrase of writers…an anthology of writers..?)

The Granite Rock

Explain that everything that is initially put on the page is just the beginning; the words are a huge granite rock waiting to be chipped into shape.

Some children may be discouraged by this as they will feel that they have written a fabulous two paragraph story, which is definitely finished because they have written *The End*, but in general students do respond well to the sculpting analogy. (You can further explain that the first draft of a story is like going to a restaurant and being presented with uncooked chicken and pasta; the chef has gathered the raw ingredients but must now follow the steps to create a first class meal!)

In the first workshop you will be introducing students to the writer's tools that will help them chip their story into shape; and the good news is that each of us already possesses all the tools we need to be great writers!

Illustrating the work

Creating an illustration is another fun way to get a student to invest in his/her work, and once invested they are more likely to take the time to check for grammar, spelling and punctuation mistakes in the final edit. In addition, colouring-in is a meditative act which often allows new ideas to pop up - many creative thinkers get their best ideas when taking part in mundane activities – such as taking a shower.

What does a writer do?

A writer puts images into people's heads by describing characters, settings and story lines in a way that convinces the reader that they are real – at least for the time that they are reading.

Meet the Author

In my experience when asked to describe an author, children tend to think that apart from J.K Rowling, most authors are men, usually tie-wearing, sophisticated bearded men, smoking pipes. This image prevents many children, and adults, from believing that they are the 'writer type'.

There is no type – we are all authors when we create and polish a piece of writing, we are all published when the finished work has been read by someone else.

I use exactly the same workshops for children and adults. In the first session the children are given a worksheet and are asked to draw an author – of course I tell them they have to draw a self-portrait. With adults I ask them to bring a photograph of themselves to be used in the first session.

The Writing for Fun course is designed to build self-confidence and to bring validity to the characters and stories we create. I have developed a creative writing phrase that works well both children and adults, I tell them, "You're the boss." It is amazing how liberating this can be. Students ask can I do this…should I do that and I tell them – it's your character, it's your world – you're the boss!

The Writer's Toolbox

Ask the students to tell you what tools a writer might use; most will list pen, paper, pencil, computer, eraser, imagination, a brain and so on. All perfect answers. But the following are equally important and are the tools that will lift good writing into great writing.

Our Five Senses
Our Emotions
Our Life Experiences
Simile
Metaphor

These concepts are introduced in the first two workshops and reiterated throughout the course. The following pages contain a lesson plan for each workshop followed by worksheets for students, which you can use or adapt.

Workshops

1. What does an author look like? Writing tools/senses

2. Writing tools/life experience/simile

3. Writing tools/simile and metaphor

4. The elements of story

5. Story shape

6. Guided story

7. Rewriting story

8. Elements of poetry and poems need shape too

9. Using simile, metaphor and life experience in poetry

The writing exercises should take 30 – 40 minutes, leaving time for each student to read out part of their work in a one hour workshop. In smaller groups more time can be dedicated to each student. Minimum times are suggested for each exercise.

The workshops are suitable for all ages. Create your own worksheets for students under the age of 8 or write headings on a board.

Words in bold in the lesson plans are to be shared with students. Non-bold sentences contain insights and extra material for the tutor.

The objective of each workshop is to foster confidence, creative thinking and expression.

Extra writing exercises in Appendix 1.

Examples of descriptive writing Appendix 2.

Editing as you write is like pressing the brake pedal while you drive.
Denise Howie

Lesson Plan Workshop 1:
Authors / Writing Tools / Senses

Extra Materials

Mandarin oranges (or satsumas or tangerines). Enough for one shared between 1 – 3 students.

1. Authors (5 – 10 mins.)

What does an author look like? What kind of people are they?

DISCUSSION. The students can call out the answers and there's no pressure to write anything down yet. All answers are okay (as long as they are within your boundaries of acceptable language etc.) they are describing their world view as it is at this present time – or they are showing off to you and their peers, but that's okay too, you will help them harness the silliness into a great story!

This is what an author looks like… Ask the students to draw a self-portrait. Emphasise that writers are ordinary people.

2. The Writer's Toolbox (5 -10 mins.)

a) List the tools that a writer uses.

Most will list pen, paper, pencil, computer, eraser, imagination, a brain and so on.
All great answers! But our senses are equally important and are tools that will lift good writing into great writing

b) List the five senses

3. The Mandarin Orange Exercise (15 - 20mins.)

Give students a small mandarin orange (and paper towel!).

Write a two or three sentence description of the orange.

The students can read out their descriptions. Most will describe its properties – its colour, its shape and some will say it's squishy or describe the smell. All great answers!

Now look at the surface closely – describe what it looks like – what it reminds you of.

If the students are struggling tell them what you think the mandarin skin looks like – an old leather boot for example. There is no incorrect answer.

Peel the mandarin and examine the pieces of skin – what does the underside look like? What does it feel like?

If they describe the properties acknowledge the answer as being correct then ask them to use their other writing tools their senses and their life experiences to describe the mandarin – what is it like – what does it remind them of?

What does the smell remind you of?
(A foreign country? Packed lunches?)
What memory does it evoke?
(Shaky old great-grandma dabbing perfume on her wrists? Opening your Christmas stocking?)

What about taste?

Does the orange make sounds?
This could get messy!

<u>Summarise</u>
Compare the original descriptions – round, orange, fat, hard, to the later ones in which the students used their 5 senses to find richer descriptions and perhaps some creative mini-stories.

Note: You could repeat this workshop halfway through the course, using chocolate or some other treat to add to the fun factor.

The accompanying student worksheet is on page 44. Simply photocopy as many as you need.

Wise Words One

"There is nothing to writing. All you do is sit down at a typewriter and bleed." Ernest Hemingway

"A story is a letter that the author writes to himself, to tell himself things that he would be unable to discover otherwise." Carlos R Zafon

"Two hours of writing fiction leaves this writer completely drained. For those two hours he has been in a different place with totally different people." Roald Dahl

"There is no greater agony than bearing an untold story inside you." Maya Angelou

"If you don't have time to read, you don't have the time (or the tools) to write. Simple as that." Stephen King

"How vain it is to sit down to write when you have not stood up to live." Henry David Thoreau

"Write the kind of story you would like to read. People will give you all sorts of advice about writing, but if you are not writing something you like, no one else will like it either." Meg Cabot

"I love deadlines. I love the whooshing noise they make as they go by." Douglas Adams

"There are three rules for writing a novel. Unfortunately, no one knows what they are." W. Somerset Maugham

"You can't wait for inspiration. You have to go after it with a club." Jack London

Lesson Plan Workshop 2:
Writing Tools: Life Experience / Simile

1. Recap Senses

When you use words (descriptive language) to appeal to one or more of the five senses: touch, sight, hearing, smell and taste you are using imagery. Imagery gives readers an immediate sense of the world you have created.

2. Emotions (2 – 5 mins.)

List some emotions

Students can write or call out answers.

3. As a writer you will be given the advice "write what you know." (8 – 12 mins.)

Read out or paraphrase the following points.

Does JK Rowling know actual wizards? Did she ever go to the Hogwarts School of Witchcraft and Wizardry?

Have authors who write about space travel or dragons ever been in to space or met a dragon?

So, what do these authors' know? They know their life-experiences.
You know YOUR life-experiences.
You probably haven't been face to face with a snarling lion, but you will remember how you felt when you were scared or something startled you, even if it was just in a dream. You have probably seen a cat creeping stealthily and crouching to jump. You may have jumped when a barking dog launched itself at a fence as you walked by. You may not have been to Africa or India, but you have felt the hot sun on your skin, you know the smell of flowers, you have heard birds sing. You are fully equipped to write about a frightening experience with a lion!

DISCUSSION: Students can share examples of everyday experiences that could be used to create a dramatic story.

You know your life-experiences, senses and emotions, which means you already own most of the tools in the Writer's Toolbox!

4. Simile Exercise (10 – 15 mins.)

When we say something is like something else we are using a simile - the full moon is LIKE a silver wheel

Or when we use *as* – his hands were *as* cold as ice

When you hear a simile you immediately see an image in your mind – a picture of big silver wheel in the night sky, or white frozen hands for example.

Think of and write down more ways to describe the moon – say what it is like.
(A pickled onion, a button, an eye, a fingernail, a door knob, a balloon…)

The sky is like
(An umbrella, a blue baby blanket, a snow globe, a black curtain…)

The Ocean is like
(A giant bath, a mirror, an angry monster, a puddle of tears…)

It seems simple, but simile is an important tool in the craft of writing.

Remember that it is important for students to share their ideas with the class.

 6. The Martian Exercise (8 – 12mins.)

Explain how the story idea is a rock that the students can chip into shape later with their writer's tools. This is what makes the difference between good writing and GREAT writing!

The first draft is just the opportunity to tell yourself the story.

Pretend you are an alien from Mars. You arrive on Earth and see a fizzy drink; how would you describe it to your fellow Martians when you get back to your own planet? Remember they have never seen it before – as the alien you will have to tell everyone back on Mars what it is like, using simile to put images in their heads (instead of describing the physical properties). Remember to use all your senses.

For example, it looks like cold lava bubbling upwards, it feels like tiny arrows hitting my nose, it tastes as sweet as finding a planet when you are lost, it sounds like a colony of ants marching on ice, it smells like the breath of a honey bee.

Some students may make reference to made-up comparisons from the alien's own planet, which is good too!

How would the alien describe:

Smoke
Snow
Cats

Students may slip between simile and metaphor in this exercise. If so, point out that metaphor is equally important, and you will be using more in the next lesson.

<u>Summarise</u>
Write what you know: You don't have to live an extraordinary life to be able to write well. If you take notice of the ordinary details around you and use your senses and memories you will discover that you know a great deal more than you thought.

Descriptive language: As a writer it is fun to find creative ways to describe objects, people and events plus it makes the piece more interesting for the reader.

Find examples of Descriptive Writing in Appendix Two

Note: You could give each student a glass of pop/soda at the beginning of the exercise.

The accompanying student worksheet is on page 46. Simply photocopy as many as you need.

Lesson Plan Workshop 3:
Simile and Metaphor

1. Recap the writer's tools so far. (1-2 mins.)
Senses
Emotions
Life Experiences
Simile

2. Simile and Metaphor (10 - 15mins.)
As with simile we use metaphor to put an image into the head of the reader or listener by comparing one thing with another, but without using *like* or *as*.

Simile:
His heart was as hard AS stone.
His heart was LIKE a stone

Metaphor:
He had a heart of stone.
His heart was carved from stone.
His stone heart shattered when he heard her words.

Examples of Simile

All the Colours of the Earth by Sheila Hamanaka

Children come with hair like bouncy baby lambs

… hair that flows like water,

…hair curls like sleeping cats in snoozy cat colours

Miz Berlin Walks by Jane Yolen

…her hair was white and fine
like the fluff of a dandelion

Quick as a Cricket by Audrey Wood

I'm as quick as a cricket,
I'm as slow as a snail.
I'm as small as an ant,
I'm as large as a whale.

Examples of Metaphor

You're a Mean One, Mr. Grinch by Dr. Seuss

You're a foul one, Mr. Grinch.
You're a nasty, wasty skunk.
Your heart is full of unwashed socks
Your soul is full of gunk.

Dr Xargle's Book of Earthlets by Jeanne Willis

(De Xargle is an alien. He is describing babies.)

"Good Morning class. Today we are going to learn about Earthlets.

They come in four colors. Pink, brown, black or yellow...but not green. They have one head and only two eyes, two short tentacles with pheelers on the end and two long tentacles called leggies.

They have square claws, which they use to frighten off wild beasts known as Tibbles and Marmaduke. Earthlets grow fur on their head but not enough to keep them warm. They must be wrapped in the hairdo of a sheep."

3. The students will read over the Martian Exercise from workshop 2 and develop it into a story – some may say that they are happy with what they have already written - remind them of the sculpting analogy! One or two may have been so enthused that they went away and finished the story – ask them to go over it one more time to add metaphor, and if they have time they can start another story.

 Martian Story (20 -25 mins.)

In the Martian exercise you created a rock boulder and started giving it shape, now it's time to chisel away with your writer tools and add all the fine details

You are the Martian. Using the writer's tools write about your experience of landing on Earth for the first time. Everything is totally different from back home on Mars so you don't know what anything is called.

You will have to describe what you see using simile and metaphor – images. Tell your fellow Martians what Earth and Earth things are like.

You can use the material you put together in the Martian Exercise - pop, smoke, snow, a cat or anything you want. You are creating the world that the Martian is seeing.

<u>Prompts:</u> Where did the Martian land – country – town – city? Describe the first five things the Martian sees (using simile or metaphor). How does he/she feel?

<u>Summarise</u>
Simile & Metaphor: Authors that use imagery give the reader the tools to help him or her to imagine the scene as though he or she is actually experiencing the place, time and events of the scene.

First Drafts: First drafts of stories and poems are not meant to be perfect; they are the rock waiting to be sculpted into shape.

The accompanying student worksheet is on page 48. Simply photocopy as many as you need.

Wise Words Two

"Good writing is supposed to evoke sensation in the reader - not the fact that it's raining, but the feel of being rained upon." E.L. Doctorow

"Memories establish the past; Senses perceive the present; Imaginations shape the future." Toba Beta

"Nothing exists in the intellect that has not first gone through the senses." Plutarch

"The five senses are the ministers of the soul." Leonardo da Vinci

"What lies behind us and what lies before us are tiny matters, compared to what lies within us." Ralph Waldo Emerson

"The true mystery of the world is the visible, not the invisible." Oscar Wilde

"A little talent is a good thing to have if you want to be a writer. But the only real requirement is the ability to remember every scar." Stephen King

Lesson Plan Workshop 4:
The Elements of Story

1. What is a story? (10 – 15 mins)
A story is a chain of events that begins in one place and ends in another. Story follows one or more character's journey through the events. At the end the reader should be able to see the purpose or meaning of the story.

2. The basic elements of story are:

Characters - the people, animals or creatures that take part in the story.

Setting - where and when the story takes place. The story can take place in the past, present or future, or any combination of the three. The setting can be a real place, or an imaginary one. The story can take place in just one place, or in many, it's up to you – you're the boss!

Plot - the sequence of events in a story. The events must be linked, creating an explanation of 'why' things happen. A classic example is, "The king died and then the queen died," is NOT a plot. Whilst "The king died and then the queen died of grief," IS a plot because there is a causal chain of events.

Plot contains - story beginning, middle and end.

Conflict – the plot needs **problems** and events that lead to **solutions**.

Resolution – what happened to the characters after the problems were (or were not) solved?

Theme is the meaning behind or revealed by the story, the main idea that a writer is trying to convey, 'if at first you don't succeed, try and try again' or 'believe in yourself' for example.

In the same way that using simile/metaphor/senses/emotions and experiences will help the reader to identify with your story, a theme also makes the story seem real to the reader as it contains a message that they recognize from real life, even if the story is about talking pigs or time machines.

Many writers do not to start out with a theme in mind, but after reading the story a theme can be found and strengthened in the next draft.

4. When I left Home This Morning Exercise (20-25 mins)

a) Write one or two sentences for each question.

Imagine that you are heading towards your front door as you leave to go to school. Describe what you see, hear, smell.

Pick your backpack up from the floor or take it down from a coat hook.

Using simile or metaphor, describe what the front door looks like - The door looks like a white chocolate bar for example. See how this puts an image in the reader's head?

Reach out and touch the door handle, how does it feel in your hand? Cold, warm? Smooth, rough?

Describe turning the handle to open the door.

Describe opening the door, how does it feel? What sound does it make? What does the sound remind you of?

Describe walking out of the door and what you see.

Describe walking to the gate. What do you see, smell, and hear? How does it make you feel?

b) Now rewrite the answers as if you were:

A three year old child, remember your height will be different, you won't have the same strength.

OR as if you were floating in the air towards the door.

OR as if you were 100 years old.

This works best if you go through the questions again.

Summarise
The writers' job is to make the story seem real for the reader for the time that he or she is reading it. Stories are built from specific elements. The writer is in complete control of the story; he/she can change its direction and outcome.

The accompanying student worksheet is on page 50. Simply photocopy as many as you need.

Lesson Plan Workshop 5:
Story Shape

1. Story Shape (10 - 15 mins)
Stories are shaped like Santa – that is, the fattest part is in the middle. This is where the problems that your character comes up against take place.

Remember ALL stories have a problem that has to be solved. Think about every story you have heard, read or seen and you will see that this is true!

For example: The Three Little Pigs, Captain Underpants, Moby Dick, Huckleberry Finn, Life of Pi, Tom and Jerry…

Beginning
Characters & Setting - who, where and when
Where is your character going? What do they want? What is their goal? To be team captain? To save the world? To get home in time for supper?

Middle – The fattest part
Problems and how solved. A problem is anything that is stopping the character reaching his/her goal. The barrier can be internal (the character's fears or over confidence for example) or external (another person or a savage storm…).
The character must play a part in solving the problem – it can't just be a stroke of luck.

End
The overall solution. How did it end up? Has the character or situation changed or is everything just the same? What did the character learn? What has the reader learned?

2. Take a short cut to chipping your story into shape!

Once you have an idea for a character or an event, it can be useful to think about how the story might end. You can always change the end later if you want – after all, it's your story!

Think of a story idea and then write three headings, Beginning, Middle, End and fill them in with your story outline.

Example:

Beginning – Three pigs leave home to build their own houses. Their mother warns them to keep safe.

Middle – The brothers have problems with a hungry wolf. First he destroys one lazy brother's house, which is made from straw – then the other, which is made from twigs but they manage to escape and run to the safety of their brother's house.

End – The wolf cannot blow down the third brother's house because he had planned ahead and worked hard to build his house with bricks. In the end the siblings work together to get rid of the wolf for ever and are able to live in peace.

3. What themes can you see in The Three Little Pigs?
Build a strong foundation, plan ahead, work hard, importance of family, bullies don't prosper, make smart choices, always listen to your mother...

 4. Plan and write a short story
(20 – 25 mins)

Your story plan:

Beginning
Middle
End

Now you have a story structure to build on. Don't forget to create a Santa shape – some problems in the middle. You might even be able to spot a theme to work with but don't worry if you don't – it will emerge later!

Remember to incorporate skills from the writer's tool box: Senses, Emotions, Life Experiences, Simile, and Metaphor.

Summarise
It is easier to plan your route through your story if you know the destination – how it ends. Some writers do this all the time, some writers' plan some of the time and others don't want to know where the story will end when they set off, but it is a useful exercise and it does help to have at least a vague idea of what the ending might be.

The accompanying student worksheet is on page 51. Simply photocopy as many as you need.

Lesson Plan Workshop 6:
Guided Story

 2. Forest Story Exercise (30 – 35 mins)

Guided Forest Story. Allow approximately 10 minutes for the first section of questions.

It is a bright sunny day and you are stood at the edge of a forest
Imagine you look to the left – what do you see?
Now walk into the forest – how does the ground feel beneath your feet? (You are wearing shoes).
What can you hear?
What is that smell? It triggers a memory – what is it?
Look up – what do you see?
There is an odd shaped tree – what does it look like – use simile
Sit down – how does the ground feel under your bare hands?
Something suddenly flits past you – how does it make you feel?
Continue on your journey – you come to a clearing and see a house what does it look like?
How do you feel about finding the house?
Describe the door – reach out and touch the door handle – describe it – use simile
Open the door – how does it feel – what do you hear – smell?
You enter the house. What do you see and hear?
Head up the stairs – describe the pictures on the walls.
Describe the box on the table in the first upstairs room.

(Allow 10 - 15 minutes for this section)
Soon there is a problem. What is it? How do you feel? How do you solve the problem?   What is the next problem? How do you solve it?
And the biggest and final problem?

(Allow 5 – 10 mins for this section)
You are back outside (or wherever your story led you). Now what? Where do you go now?
What did you learn on your journey through the forest and the house?
What did you learn about yourself by facing the problems?

Summarise
Writers always ask themselves questions to help create characters, settings and storylines. Even though the group is answering the same questions, each will each have a unique story told in their own voice.

The accompanying student worksheet is on page 53. Simply photocopy as many as you need.

Lesson Plan Workshop 7:
Rewriting a Story

1. Forest Story Recap (5 - 10mins.)

In the beginning you described the SETTING and created images (using your writing tools). In this story you were the main CHARACTER – do you want to create a different main character? Will this change the way he/she sees and reacts to events?

Middle: PROBLEMS/CONFLICT The story is usually better if there is more than one problem – the story doesn't end when the big bad wolf cannot blow down the house of straw, or even the house of bricks – it ends when the pigs light a fire to stop the wolf from coming down the chimney.

The middle can contain good surprises alongside the bad ones

End: RESOLUTION The story should end quickly once the biggest and final problem has been resolved. Has the character or situation changed or is everything just the same? What did the character learn?

You answered the questions and used your writer's tools to create the basis of your story. It looks good – there's a beginning a middle and an end, and the character has solved problems but now it's time for the real writing – the fun part – where you can tap away at the story, even change its shape completely if you want, after all it's your world – you're the boss!

Now that you know how the story ends you can make changes to the beginning and middle so that it flows better, or you can change the ending. Continue to ask yourself questions about the character, setting and plot

Most people just rewrite at sentence level – great writers tackle the structure until it's just the shape they were aiming for! Help the student by asking questions to fill in any gaps or inconsistencies in the story line. You are not correcting their work but guiding them to notice and reshape the structure of the story.

 2. Rewrite the Forest Story (still without the Editor!) (30 -35 mins.)

Don't just re-write your answers. Smooth it out. Remember to use your senses and emotions but start as near to the first problem as possible.

Summarise
Science fiction novelist Michael Crichton: "Books are not written - they're rewritten."

The accompanying student worksheet is on page 54. Simply photocopy as many as you need.

Wise Words Three

"Fantasy is hardly an escape from reality. It's a way of understanding it."
Lloyd Alexander

"Fiction is the truth inside the lie." Stephen King

"Either write something worth reading or do something worth writing."
Benjamin Franklin

"Description begins in the writer's imagination, but should finish in the reader's."
Stephen King

"The most valuable of all talents is that of never using two words when one will do."
Thomas Jefferson

We have to continually be jumping off cliffs and developing our wings on the way down." Kurt Vonnegut

Lesson Plan Workshop 8:
Elements of poetry.
Poems need shape too

I ask my students to imagine a large painting: **The whole landscape (the villages, mountains, forests and rivers) is a novel. Zoom in to a house with a garden and you have a short story. A poem is a single flower in that garden.**

(You could bring in a picture to illustrate the idea.)

In a poem every word should be just the right word in just the right place – everything else should be cut away. The right word is strong and clear, with little or no ambiguity of meaning (unless you are aiming for ambiguity).

1. Sound and Rhythm
Sound is important in poetry. Poems do not have to rhyme but they do have to a have rhythm - repeated patterns of sound. We automatically use rhythm when we speak and write but when we write poetry we make a point of noticing and using it.

2. Syllables (15 – 20 mins.)

Syllables are a great writer's tool!

Syllables are speech sounds. Each time you change the shape of your mouth when saying a word, you are using a new syllable.

How many syllables are there in your name?

Growing Poem 1,2,3,4,5 syllables

Look!
I see
A brown bear
Catching salmon
In the cold river

Write a Growing Poem
Haiku 5,7,5 syllables

A caramel bear
With razor claws spears salmon.
Nature's restaurant

Write a Haiku – it does not have to be the same theme as the previous poem.

Cinquain 2,4,6,8,2 syllables

Listen
A tawny bear
With razor claws and jaws
Slices through the river seeking
Dinner

Write a Cinquain – it does not have to be the same theme as the previous poems.

Counting syllable trains the writer to use the right words in the right place.

2. More Haiku (2 - 5 mins.)

Step 1: Think about a theme for your haiku, *Night* for example.

Then brainstorm the words that come to mind - bedtime – dark – owls - hidden – scary – stars –pretty…

 Step 2: Write three sentences. (5 mins.)

In the first, set the scene -   The night is so dark it's like being shut in a dark room or a box

In the second record an action or thought - The twinkling stars remind me of diamonds or eyes

The last line sums up your feelings and the mood of the poem – I like stars – they're so mysterious and pretty.

 Step 3: Chisel your ideas into three lines (5 – 10 mins)

5 syllables
7 syllables
5 syllables

Keep it simple and just express one mood or emotion.

Night is a deep box
Many eyes peep from within
I love the starlight

OR
Night is a curtain
Puncture marks reveal the light
Ever wonder why?

<u>Prompts</u> Ideas for Haiku
Rain in the street, a moment of anger, an animal moving, laughter, a bird on a telephone wire, a mountain, tears, waiting for spring, a sound, bubbles, dragons, giving thanks.

The accompanying student worksheet is on page 55. Simply photocopy as many as you need.

Lesson Plan Workshop 9:
Simile, Metaphor and Life Experience

1. Simile in Poetry (10 – 15 mins.)

Ondaatje's poem was inspired by a quote from Paul Bowles, "The Sinhalese are beyond a doubt one of the least musical people in the world. It would be quite impossible to have less sense of pitch, line or rhythm."

Sweet Like a Crow by Michael Ondaatje

Your voice sounds like a scorpion being pushed
through a glass tube
like someone has just trod on a peacock
like wind howling in a coconut
like a rusty bible, like someone pulling barbed wire
across a stone courtyard, like a pig drowning,
a vattacka being fried
a bone shaking hands
a frog singing at Carnegie Hall…

Write a simile poem.

Prompts
The poem could be about one aspect of a person – voice, eyes, hair or it could be describing the whole person.
You could describe an animal using simile.
A place.
Or an emotion.

2. Life experience in poetry. (20 – 25 mins.)

(Inspired by the poem 1950's by New Zealand poet Bill Manhire.)

My paper dolls. My fish and chips
My Tiny Tears. My pick-up sticks
My invisible horse. My invisible friend
My den. My castle. Days without end.
Snakes and ladders. Etch-a-sketch
Sindy. Trolls. Dogs playing fetch.
My hula hoop. My magic wand
My tiddley-winks. A stinky pond.

The Secret Seven. The Famous Five
Swallows and Amazons. The Call of the Wild.
My roller skates. My spinning top
Hopscotch. Elastics. Parachute drop
Pink school milk. Climbing trees
My fishing net. Scabs on knees
Whist. Gin Rummy. Memory games
Rosehips. Brambles. Country lanes.

Poetry works best if it is sparse and specific (a single rose in a landscape).
If a poem means something to the writer it will mean something to the reader.

a) Brainstorm a list of childhood toys and activities

b) Compose a poem using just things from the list – no adjectives, similes or metaphors.

Use 'my' as often as you can to show that it isn't just a random list of items from that time frame.

Play with the order that you put the sentences down, say them out loud until you find a natural rhythm.

Having to make the poem rhyme will force the students to dredge their memories for other things and events.

Short sentences and specific images will create a fast-paced dynamic poem.

Summarise
Author and humourist, Mark Twain: "The difference between the right word and the almost right word is the difference between lightning and a lightning bug."

The accompanying student worksheet is on page 57. Simply photocopy as many as you need.

Wise Words Four

"Poetry is a packsack of invisible keepsakes." Carl Sandburg

"Most of the basic material a writer works with is acquired before the age of fifteen."
Willa Cather

"Poetry is when an emotion has found its thought and the thought has found words."
Robert Frost

"Poetry is not only dream and vision; it is the skeleton architecture of our lives. It lays the foundations for a future of change, a bridge across our fears of what has never been before." Audre Lorde

"A poet's work is to name the unnameable, to point at frauds, to take sides, start arguments, shape the world, and stop it going to sleep." Salman Rushdie

"Poetry is a way of taking life by the throat." Robert Frost

Workshop Objectives

1. What does the author look like? Writing tools / senses

Objective:

To inform students that by the act of writing they become a writer/author

To show students that they already possess many of the skills of a great writer

To demonstrate how to easily develop those skills

Overview

1. What does an author look like? What kind of people are they?
2. What tools does a writer use?

Pen, paper, computer etc.

Senses (Descriptive writing.)

Life experience

3. Finding inspiration in everyday objects
4. Opportunities for class discussion

2. Writing tools / life experience / simile

Objective:

To remind the students of the importance of using descriptive language to create imagery. (Senses.)

To encourage students to incorporate figures of speech (simile) into their writing.

To show that however young the student is, he or she can emulate successful authors and draw on their own life-experiences to craft great stories or poems.

To introduce or reinforce the concept that the first draft is not the final draft.

Overview

1. Recap of the 5 senses and descriptive language.
2. The real meaning of 'write what you know'.
3. Emotion and life-experiences as writers' tools.
4. Explaining and using simile
5. Looking at everyday objects from a different perspective
6. The Granite Rock concept – the first draft is not the final draft.
7. Opportunities for class discussion
8. Opportunities to share writing

3. Writing tools / life experience / simile and metaphor

Objective:
To encourage students to incorporate figures of speech (simile and metaphor) into their writing
For students to recognise when authors are using simile and metaphor
To reinforce the concept that the first draft is not the final draft

Overview
1. Recap of the writer's tools
Senses
Emotions
Life experience
Simile
2. Introducing metaphor
3. Examples of simile and metaphor from literature
4. Writing a story based on the Martian Exercise (Looking at everyday objects and events from a different perspective.)
5. Opportunities for class discussion
6. Opportunities to share writing

4. The elements of story

Objective:
For students to be aware that all stories have structure
For students to be aware that there is a connection between the writer and the reader
To encourage students to play with their writing

Overview
1. What is a story?
2. The basic elements of story:
Beginning, middle, end.
Characters
Setting
Plot/Conflict/Solution
Resolution
Theme
3. A guided story beginning
4. Writing a scene from a different perspective
5. Opportunities for class discussion
6. Opportunities to share writing

5. Story shape

Objective:
To introduce the importance of conflict and theme
To encourage students to see the story as a whole
To show students that they can control the direction of their story

Overview
1. Story shape and conflict/resolution
2. Beginning, middle and end in story
3. Planning and writing a story
4. Theme in story
5. Opportunities for class discussion
6. Opportunities to share writing

6. Guided Story

Objective:
To learn how to generate story ideas
To practise using senses and emotions in story
To encourage students to see the story as a whole
To show students that they have their own unique voice

Overview
1. Guided story – students write down answers to questions
2. Story shape and conflict/resolution
3. Beginning, middle and end in story
4. Theme in story
5. Each writer has their own unique voice
6. Opportunities for class discussion
7. Opportunities to share writing

7. Rewriting story

Objective:
To reinforce the importance of story shape
To reinforce the importance of conflict in story
To show the effectiveness of rewriting

Overview
1. Story shape and conflict/resolution
2. Beginning, middle and end in story
3. Rewrite the existing story
4. Opportunities for class discussion
5. Opportunities to share writing

8. Elements of poetry / poems need shape too

Objective:
For students to understand what makes a poem
To understand the usefulness of syllables in structuring a poem.
For students to recognise that their experiences and perceptions have value

Overview
1. The right word in the right place
2. Syllable poems
3. Haiku
4. Opportunities for class discussion
5. Opportunities to share writing

9. Using simile, metaphor and life experience in poetry

Objective:
To practise using simile
To concentrate on using the right words
To reinforce the concept that the student's experiences and perceptions have value

Overview
1. Example of a simile poem
2. Write a simile poem
3. Example of using childhood items and places in a poem
4. Writing a childhood poem – using rhyme.
5. Opportunities for class discussion
6. Opportunities to share writing

Student Worksheets

1. **What does an author look like? Writing tools/senses**

2. **Writing tools/life experience/simile**

3. **Writing tools/simile and metaphor**

4. **The elements of story**

5. **Story shape**

6. **Guided story**

7. **Rewriting story**

8. **Elements of poetry and poems need shape too**

9. **Using simile, metaphor and life experience in poetry**

Don't tell me the moon is shining;
show me the glint of light on broken glass.
Anton Checkov

Student Worksheet 1: Authors and their writing tools

1. What does an author look like? What kind of people are they?

This is what an author looks like…

2. The Writer's Tool Box.

a) List the tools that a writer uses.

b) List the 5 senses

3. Mandarin Orange Exercise

Student Worksheet 2: Writing Tools: Life Experience / Simile

1. Recap Senses.

When you use words (descriptive language) to appeal to one or more of the five senses: touch, sight, hearing, smell and taste you are using imagery. Imagery gives readers an immediate sense of the world you have created.

2. Emotions

List some emotions

3. As a writer you will be given the advice "write what you know."

Does JK Rowling know actual wizards? Did she ever go to the Hogwarts School of Witchcraft and Wizardry?
Have authors who write about space travel or dragons ever been in to space or met a dragon?

So, what do these authors' know? They know their life-experiences.
You know YOUR life-experiences.
You probably haven't been face to face with a snarling lion, but you will remember how you felt when you were scared or something startled you, even if it was just in a dream. You have probably seen a cat creeping stealthily and crouching to jump. You may have jumped when a barking dog launched itself at a fence as you walked by. You may not have been to Africa or India, but you have felt the hot sun on your skin, you know the smell of flowers, you have heard birds sing. You are fully equipped to write about a frightening experience with a lion!

You know your life-experiences, senses and emotions, which means you already own most of the tools in the Writer's Toolbox!

4. Simile Exercise

When we say something is like something else we are using a simile - the full moon is LIKE a silver wheel

Or when we use as – his hands were AS cold as ice

When you hear a simile you immediately see an image in your mind – a picture of big silver wheel in the night sky, or white frozen hands for example.

Think of and write down more ways to describe the moon – say what it is like.

The sky is like

The Ocean is like

It seems simple, but simile is an important tool in the craft of writing.

6. The Martian Exercise

Pretend you are an alien from Mars. You arrive on Earth and see a fizzy drink; how would you describe it to your fellow Martians when you get back to your own planet? Remember they have never seen it before – as the alien you will have to tell everyone back on Mars what it is like, using simile to put images in their heads (instead of describing the physical properties). Remember to use all your senses.

How would the alien describe:

Smoke

Snow

Cats

Student Worksheet 3: Simile and Metaphor

1. Recap the writer's tools so far.

1.
2.
3.
4.

2. Simile and Metaphor
As with simile we use metaphor to put an image into the head of the reader or listener by comparing one thing with another without using like or as.

Simile:
His heart was as hard AS stone.
His heart was LIKE a stone

Metaphor:
He had a heart of stone.
His heart was carved from stone.
His stone heart shattered when he heard her words.

Examples of Simile

All the Colours of the Earth by Sheila Hamanaka

Children come with hair like bouncy baby lambs

… hair that flows like water,

…hair curls like sleeping cats in snoozy cat colours

Miz Berlin Walks by Jane Yolen

…her hair was white and fine
like the fluff of a dandelion

Quick as a Cricket by Audrey Wood

I'm as quick as a cricket,
I'm as slow as a snail.
I'm as small as an ant,
I'm as large as a whale.

Examples of Metaphor

You're a Mean One, Mr. Grinch by Dr. Seuss

You're a foul one, Mr. Grinch.
You're a nasty, wasty skunk.
Your heart is full of unwashed socks
Your soul is full of gunk.

Dr Xargle's Book of Earthlets by Jeanne Willis

(De Xargle is an alien. He is describing babies.)

"Good Morning class. Today we are going to learn about Earthlets.

They come in four colors. Pink, brown, black or yellow…but not green. They have one head and only two eyes, two short tentacles with pheelers on the end and two long tentacles called leggies.

They have square claws, which they use to frighten off wild beasts known as Tibbles and Marmaduke. Earthlets grow fur on their head but not enough to keep them warm. They must be wrapped in the hairdo of a sheep."

 3. Martian Story

In the Martian exercise you created a rock boulder and started giving it shape, now it's time to chisel away with your writer tools and add all the fine details

You are the Martian. Using the writer's tools write about your experience of landing on Earth for the first time. Everything is totally different from back home on Mars so you don't know what anything is called.

You will have to describe what you see using simile and metaphor – images. Tell your fellow Martians what Earth and Earth things are like.

You can use the material you put together in the Martian Exercise - pop, smoke, snow, a cat or anything you want. You are creating the world that the Martian is seeing.

Student Worksheet 4: The Elements of Story

1. What is a story?

A story is a chain of events that begins in one place and ends in another. Story follows one or more character's journey through the events. At the end the reader should be able to see the purpose or meaning of the story.

2. The basic elements of story are:

Characters - the people, animals or creatures that take part in the story.

Setting - where and when the story takes place. The story can take place in the past, present or future, or any combination of the three. The setting can be a real place, or an imaginary one. The story can take place in just one place, or in many, it's up to you – you're the boss!

Plot - the sequence of events in a story. The events must be linked, creating an explanation of 'why' things happen. A classic example is, "The king died and then the queen died," is NOT a plot. Whilst "The king died and then the queen died of grief," IS a plot because there is a causal chain of events.

Plot contains - story beginning, middle and end.

Conflict – the plot needs **problems** and events that lead to **solutions**.

Resolution – what happened to the characters after the problems were (or were not) solved?

Theme is the meaning behind or revealed by the story, the main idea that a writer is trying to convey, 'if at first you don't succeed, try and try again' or 'believe in yourself' for example.

Many writers do not to start out with a theme in mind, but after reading the story a theme can be found and strengthened in the next draft.

 4. When I left Home This Morning Exercise

a) On a separate sheet, write one or two sentences for each question.

b) Now rewrite the answers as if you were:

Student Worksheet 5: Story Shape

1. Story Shape
Stories are shaped like Santa – that is, the fattest part is in the middle. This is where the problems that your character comes up against take place.

Remember ALL stories have a problem that has to be solved. Think about every story you have heard, read or seen and you will see that this is true!

For example: The Three Little Pigs, Captain Underpants, Moby Dick, Huckleberry Finn, Life of Pi, Tom and Jerry…

Beginning
Characters & Setting - who, where and when
Where is your character going? What do they want? What is their goal? To be team captain? To save the world? To get home in time for supper?

Middle – The fattest part
Problems and how solved. A problem is anything that is stopping the character reaching his/her goal. The barrier can be internal (the character's fears or over confidence for example) or external (another person or a savage storm…).
The character must play a part in solving the problem – it can't just be a stroke of luck.

End
The overall solution. How did it end up? Has the character or situation changed or is everything just the same? What did the character learn? What has the reader learned?

2. Take a short cut to chipping your story into shape!

Once you have an idea for a character or an event, it can be useful to think about how the story might end. You can always change the end later if you want – after all, it's your story!

Think of a story idea and then write three headings, Beginning, Middle, End and fill them in with your story outline.

Example:

Beginning – Three pigs leave home to build their own houses. Their mother warns them to keep safe.

Middle – The brothers have problems with a hungry wolf. First he destroys one lazy brother's house, which is made from straw – then the other, which is made from twigs but they manage to escape and run to the safety of their brother's house.

End – The wolf cannot blow down the third brother's house because he had planned ahead and worked hard to build his house with bricks. In the end the siblings work together to get rid of the wolf for ever and are able to live in peace.

3. What themes can you see in The Three Little Pigs?

 4. Plan and write a short story (20 – 25 mins)

Your story plan:

Beginning

Middle

End

Now you have a story structure to build on. Don't forget to create a Santa shape – some problems in the middle. You might even be able to spot a theme to work with but don't worry if you don't – it will emerge later!

Remember to incorporate skills from the writer's tool box: Senses, Emotions, Life Experiences, Simile, and Metaphor.

Student Worksheet 6: Guided Story

 2. Forest Story Exercise

Student Worksheet 7: Rewriting a Story

1. Forest Story Recap

In the beginning you described the SETTING and created images (using your writing tools). In this story you were the main CHARACTER – do you want to create a different main character? Will this change the way he/she sees and reacts to events?

Middle: PROBLEMS/CONFLICT The story is usually better if there is more than one problem – the story doesn't end when the big bad wolf cannot blow down the house of straw, or even the house of bricks – it ends when the pigs light a fire to stop the wolf from coming down the chimney.

The middle can contain good surprises alongside the bad ones

End: RESOLUTION The story should end quickly once the biggest and final problem has been resolved. Has the character or situation changed or is everything just the same? What did the character learn?

You answered the questions and used your writer's tools to create the basis of your story. It looks good – there's a beginning a middle and an end, and the character has solved problems but now it's time for the real writing – the fun part – where you can tap away at the story, even change its shape completely if you want, after all it's your world – you're the boss!

Now that you know how the story ends you can make changes to the beginning and middle so that it flows better, or you can change the ending. Continue to ask yourself questions about the character, setting and plot

 ### 2. Rewrite the Forest Story

Don't just re-write your answers. Smooth it out. Remember to use your senses and emotions but start as near to the first problem as possible.

Student Worksheet 8: Elements of Poetry. Poems need shape too

Imagine a large painting: The whole landscape (the villages, mountains, forests and rivers) is a novel. Zoom in to a house with a garden and you have a short story. A poem is a single flower in that garden.

1. Sound and Rhythm
Sound is important in poetry. Poems do not have to rhyme but they do have to a have rhythm - repeated patterns of sound. We automatically use rhythm when we speak and write but when we write poetry we make a point of noticing and using it.

2. Syllables

Syllables are a great writer's tool!

Syllables are speech sounds. Each time you change the shape of your mouth when saying a word, you are using a new syllable.

How many syllables are there in your name?

Growing Poem (1,2,3,4,5 syllables)

Look!
I see
A brown bear
Catching salmon
In the cold river

Write a Growing Poem

Haiku (5,7,5 syllables)

A caramel bear
With razor claws spears salmon.
Nature's restaurant

Write a Haiku – it does not have to be the same theme as the previous poem.

Cinquain (2,4,6,8,2 syllables)

Listen
A tawny bear
With razor claws and jaws
Slices through the river seeking
Salmon

Write a Cinquain – it does not have to be the same theme as the previous poems.

Using a syllable-count trains the writer to use the right words in the right place.

2. More Haiku

Step 1: Think about a theme for your haiku Night for example.

Then brainstorm the words that come to mind - bedtime – dark – owls - hidden – scary – stars –pretty…

 Step 2: Write three sentences.

   In the first, set the scene -   The night is so dark it's like being shut in a dark room or a box

In the second record an action or thought - The twinkling stars remind me of diamonds or eyes

The last line sums up your feelings and the mood of the poem – I like stars – they're so mysterious and pretty.

Step 3: Chisel your ideas into three lines

5 syllables
7 syllables
5 syllables

Keep it simple and just express one mood or emotion.

Night is a deep box
Many eyes peep from within
I love the starlight

OR

Night is a curtain
Puncture marks reveal the light
Ever wonder why?

Student Worksheet 9: Simile, Metaphor and Life Experience

1. Simile in Poetry

Ondaatje's poem was inspired by a quote from Paul Bowles, "The Sinhalese are beyond a doubt one of the least musical people in the world. It would be quite impossible to have less sense of pitch, line or rhythm."

Sweet Like a Crow by Michael Ondaatje

Your voice sounds like a scorpion being pushed
through a glass tube
like someone has just trod on a peacock
like wind howling in a coconut
like a rusty bible, like someone pulling barbed wire
across a stone courtyard, like a pig drowning,
a vattacka being fried
a bone shaking hands
a frog singing at Carnegie Hall…

Write a simile poem.

2. Life experience in poetry

(Inspired by the poem 1950's by New Zealand poet Bill Manhire.)

My paper dolls. My fish and chips
My Tiny Tears. My pick-up sticks
My invisible horse. My invisible friend
My den. My castle. Days without end.
Snakes and ladders. Etch-a-sketch
Sindy. Trolls. Dogs playing fetch.
My hula hoop. My magic wand
My tiddley-winks. A stinky pond.

The Secret Seven. The Famous Five
Swallows and Amazons. The Call of the Wild.
My roller skates. My spinning top
Hopscotch. Elastics. Parachute drop
Pink school milk. Climbing trees
My fishing net. Scabs on knees
Whist. Gin Rummy. Memory games
Rosehips. Brambles. Country lanes.

Poetry works best if it is sparse and specific (a single rose in a landscape).

If a poem means something to the writer it will mean something to the reader.

a) Brainstorm a list of childhood toys and activities

b) Compose a poem using just things from the list – no adjectives, similes or metaphors.

Use 'my' as often as you can to show that it isn't just a random list of items from that time frame.

Play with the order that you put the sentences down, say them out loud until you find a natural rhythm.

Part Three

A word after a word after a word is power.
Margaret Attwood

Invite the Editor in

When the work is going to be displayed, sent off for a competition or published
If the student wishes to after the final version has taken shape

Some students may be stressed by their work not being perfect straight away, which will inhibit creativity in any case so by all means help them to edit as they go if needed.

The run through for spelling and grammar is the final polish before presenting the sculpture to a wider audience, for the purposes of this course (stimulating creativity) those reading the work should focus on the craftsmanship rather than the polish.

It's difficult for us as adults/tutors to allow writing to go unedited; especially if the students are children taking their work home but our entire academic (and personal) lives are ruled by the internal Editor so there is no risk of students permanently disregarding the mechanics of writing because of these workshops. However there is the pay-off of better writing skills and increased self-confidence.

In the workshops you have been helping the student to restructure the story or poem by asking questions to fill in any gaps or inconsistencies in the story line. The next book, Level 2, will deal with structural revision more deeply, and will provide the next step of workshops designed to build on the skills acquired here.

Dyslexia, youth and other challenges to writing.

Difficulties in reading and writing bear no relationship to the ability to be creative. In fact many creative people in history had leaning difficulties – Alexander Graham Bell, Thomas Edison, Albert Einstein, Hans Christian Anderson, Lewis Carroll and Agatha Christie for example. This may be because people who have learning difficulties tend to think in pictures and most creative thinkers also use a visual learning style.

Young children brim over with creativity (In Land's study 98% of the children scored as 'creative geniuses') but are not able to write down their ideas or stories whereas successful writers force themselves back into a childhood state – questioning the world around them and blurring the lines between fantasy and reality, possible and impossible in order to harness the innate creative genius.

Set students up for success!

Most children with reading and writing challenges will be wary of facing the frustration and possible embarrassment associated with trying to write but this course is about *story* – the joy of the new worlds, characters and possibilities we can each create – the inability to set it down on paper should never be a barrier.

Have small groups. If the group is solely made up of students with challenges I have found that 4 or less works best.

Take small breaks. People with reading and writing challenge find it difficult to concentrate for long periods of time.

Be patient with silliness. Children with dyslexia often play the class clown to postpone having to do a task, or to cover up the fact that they don't understand the assignment.

Set the ground rules. **Banish the Editor!** Remind students that spelling and handwriting are not important at this stage - writing stories is not about spelling, it is about putting mind-movies into other people's heads. (Descriptive writing examples appendix 2.)

I then mention people they may have heard of who have become successful even though they were not good at spelling or the mechanics of writing in school. (Walt Disney, Selma Hayek, Richard Branson, Whoopi Goldberg, Steve Jobs, Steven Speilberg, Anderson Cooper, Tom Cruise, Orlando Bloom. See appendix 3 for more examples.)

Work at the students' pace. Depending on ability, as you read out the questions you could have students call out their answers and you write them down (or have a workshop assistant help with this) or the student can write the answers – not worrying about tidiness or spelling. After a few minutes stop and re-read the questions and ask the students to read out the answers to you - or you read out what they have dictated to you. You will soon be able to gauge how frequently you need to stop.

Some students are adept at remembering/deciphering what they have written and others are not.

In a one-to-one workshop, the student can speak into a tape recorder.

Make it Fun! By removing the stress of having to listen an internal Editor or having to perform for an external one you are allowing the students to create stories that they can become emotionally attached to. Once they are attached to their characters and care what happens to them they are more likely to care about the finished product and be prepared to rewrite and, with help, add the final proofreading polish.

During the 'writing' process provide prompts, such as 'what happened next?' and encourage the student to ask his/her own questions of the story and characters.

When editing for a student do not be tempted to rewrite the story to make it 'better'.

Larger groups with one or two students who have challenges. It is easy to incorporate the steps above into a general workshop. I have found that students (of any age) understand and accommodate the slower pace.

Without generalizing, children who have challenges with reading and writing are often creative and witty, using their visual and aural strengths to come up with great stories to entertain the group

Too young to write?

We know that by reading to a child we foster a love of story, which creates a foundation for reading and writing. Imagine the confidence gained by a child actually publishing his or her own work!

Children as young as three can dictate a story to an adult or sibling or into a tape recorder to be transcribed later. If they get stuck provide a prompt, such as, what does the character see? Hear? How does she feel? But don't bombard them, and don't be tempted to tidy up the story as you write it out. Even young children appreciate the feeling of control in the creative process.

Common Problems with Dyslexia (and similar challenges)

Following Instructions
People who have dyslexia often have difficulty with sequencing and following instructions, the Writing For Fun workshops incorporate guided stories (the writer answers questions) and concrete examples of what is required.

Attention Span
People who have dyslexia often struggle with focussing and may be easily distracted. It is difficult for these students to listen attentively for long periods of time. The workshops can be easily broken down. Students are given frequent opportunities to share their work and ideas, and illustrations are encouraged. Many students listen more attentively when colouring in a picture!

Reading Ability
The student may not be able to read well – or at all. The workshops are designed to be read out by the tutor, and as the class will be small you can just proceed at the group's pace.

Spelling Ability
The inability to spell is a major source of frustration for people who have dyslexia – one of the criteria for diagnosing dyslexia is the mismatch between the person's intelligence and their ability to spell, read and write. Some students will be able to interpret their misspelled work and read it out to you but some will not. If students are writing rather than dictating encourage them to draw quick illustrations every few sentences to remind themselves of the story line.

Handwriting Ability
Some children with dyslexia also have dysgraphia, which makes it difficult for them to order their thoughts and to write legibly. Many children will have built up a resistance to writing because of this but you can provide alternatives to help the student share the images he has in his mind, such as dictation or using a keyboard.

Speech Abilities
The student may also have speech problems that will make her reluctant to read her work out loud. They may mispronounce words as a toddler would – 'pisgeti' instead of 'spaghetti' for example, and have trouble with words that are more than one or two syllables. They might also have difficulty retrieving the correct words when speaking or writing, leading them to resort to vague words such as 'thing' or 'stuff.' There is no pressure for a child to read out their work but it would help increase their confidence if (with their permission) you were to read it out for them - after you have gone through it with the student to make sure you aren't tripping over the incorrect spelling.

Appendix 1. Extra Writing Exercises.

Senses, Simile and Metaphor

1. Think of two linked but opposing subjects such as day/night, hope/fear, summer/winter sky/earth and ask yourself questions about each.

Touch – what does it feel like or **what do you imagine** it feels like? Soft or hard? A toasted marshmallow? Bathing in sunshine?

Sight – what does it look like? Big or small, shiny or dull. A patterned quilt? A summer pool party?

Sound – what does it sound like? Loud or quiet? A shout or a whisper? A door slamming shut in anger?

Smell – what does it smell like? Fresh or sharp? A meadow or a damp broom cupboard? Your first day of school?

Taste – what does it taste like? Bitter or sweet? Strawberries and cream or cold ashes? A farmer's old boot?

Select some of your answers and write the beginnings of a poem

Autumn feels like (a prickly pinecone in a pile of paper leaves)

Spring feels like (a plump drop of dew on the tip of my finger)

Autumn looks like (the distant V of departing geese)

Spring looks like (green lava erupting from the earth)

Autumn sounds like (a dog barking in the woods)

Spring sounds like (mountains yawning and stretching)

Autumn smells like (potatoes baking in a bonfire)

Spring smells like (a talcumed baby)

Autumn tastes like (caramel toffee apples)

Spring tastes like (tomorrow)

If you wish you can then rewrite the poem without using 'like'.
'Autumn is a prickly pinecone' for example.

Try mixing simile and metaphor.

This could end up being two poems, one about Autumn and one about Spring.

2. Story Shape

You will need a variety of colours, such as a swatch of paint samples or bundles of pencil crayons.

Give each student a colour and ask them to imagine that they are somewhere far away from home. They have been away for many years and now that they have seen this colour it reminds them of something from their old life.

What memory does the colour jog?
Put the same memory into a character. (Some students may have already answered as a character.)
What is the character's name? Male or female? How old?
Where is he or she now?
Something is preventing your character from going home. What is it? Distance? Money? Pride? Fear?
Your character is now determined to go home how does he/she solve the problem?
Describe the first half of the journey home - then add another problem.
How does your character solve this problem?
Describe the homecoming. How does she or he feel? Was it as they had expected?
Now write a beginning paragraph describing what happened to trigger your character's departure from home.

(Now or later) Read through the answers and get the storyline straight in your head and then write the story from beginning to end with the problems in the middle. You can add, change or take out elements to make it the best story it can be.

Appendix 2. Examples of Descriptive Writing

Ray Bradbury, The Halloween Tree

Behind one door, Tom Skelton, aged thirteen, stopped and listened.
The wind outside nested in each tree, prowled the sidewalks in invisible treads like unseen cats. Tom Skelton shivered. Anyone could see that the wind was a special wind this night, and the darkness took on a special feel because it was All Hallows' Eve. Everything seemed cut from soft black velvet or gold or orange velvet. Smoke panted up out of a thousand chimneys like the plumes of funeral parades. From kitchen windows drifted two pumpkin smells: gourds being cut, pies being baked.

Alexander McCall Smith, The Number 1 Detective Agency

Suddenly she saw the house, tucked away behind the trees almost in the shadow of the hill. It was a bare earth house in the traditional style; brown mud walls, a few glassless windows, with a knee-height wall around the yard. A previous owner, a long time ago, had painted designs on the wall, but neglect and the years had scaled them off and only their ghosts remained … She opened the door and eased herself out of the van. The sun was riding high; its light prickled at her skin. They were too far west here, too close to the Kalahari Desert, and her unease increased. This was not the comforting land she had grown up with; this was the merciless Africa, the waterless land.

Charles Dickens, Hard Times

He was a rich man: banker, merchant, manufacturer, and what not. A big, loud man, with a stare, and a metallic laugh. A man made out of a coarse material, which seemed to have been stretched to make so much of him. A man with a great puffed head and forehead, swelled veins in his temples, and such a strained skin to his face that it seemed to hold his eyes open, and lift his eyebrows up. A man with a pervading appearance on him of being infl ated like a balloon, and ready to start. A man who could never sufficiently vaunt himself a self-made man. A man who was always proclaiming, through that brassy speaking-trumpet of a voice of his, his old ignorance and his old poverty. A man who was the Bully of humility.

Gerald Durrell, My Family and Other Animals

Halfway up the slope, guarded by a group of tall, slim, cypress-trees, nestled a small strawberry-pink villa, like some exotic fruit lying in the greenery. The cypress-trees undulated gently in the breeze, as if they were busily painting the sky a still brighter blue for our arrival.

Appendix 3. Famous people with reading and writing difficulties.

Writers

Agatha Christie (Bestselling author of all time! Mystery Writer)
Avi (Grade Books for schools)
Dav Pilkey (Wrote Captain Underpants!)
F. Scott Fitzgerald (Billed as one of the greatest American writers)
Hans Christain Anderson (Fairy Tales & Poetry)
J F Lawton (Screenwriter)
Jules Verne (Science Fiction)
Lynda La Plante (TV Writer)
Philip Shultz (Winner of Pulitzer Prize for Poetry)
Sherrilyn Kenyon (Dark Hunter vampire series)
Stephen J Cannell (Novelist, script writer and TV producer)
WB Yeats (Poet)

Filmakers

Steven Spielberg (Co-founder of Dreamworks, director, producer, screenwriter)
Walt Disney (Founder of the Walt Disney Company, producer, director, screenwriter)

Entrepreneurs & Business Leaders

Charles Schwab (Investor)
Frank W Woolworth (Founder of Woolworths)
Henry Ford (Founder of Ford Motors)
Ingvar Kamprad (Founder of Ikea)
Richard Branson (Founder of Virgin Enterprises)
Steve Jobs (Founder of Apple)
William Hewlett (Co-founder Hewlett & Packard Computers)

Political Leaders

George Washington (1st U.S. President)
Thomas Jefferson (3rd U.S. President)
John F Kennedy (35th U.S. President)
Winston Churchill (British Prime Minister)
Nelson Rockefeller (U.S. Businessman and politician)

There are also many actors, athletes, designers, artists and architects, including Whoopi Goldberg, Bob May, Tommy Hilfiger and Leonardo de Vinci.

 Denise Howie: Author

 denisehowie.blogspot.ca

 @AuthorDHowie

 @denisehowieauthor

 denise@denisehowie.com

I would love to hear from you!

Made in the USA
Charleston, SC
03 December 2016